THE
MORROW
PLOTS

THE
MORROW
PLOTS

Poems by

Matthew Gavin Frank

BLACK LAWRENCE PRESS

Black Lawrence Press
www.blacklawrence.com

Executive Editor: Diane Goettel
Book Design: Amy Freels
Cover Design: Rebecca Maslen
Cover Art: "Determinant" by Justine Bursoni

Copyright © 2013 Matthew Gavin Frank
ISBN: 978-1-937854-27-0

All rights reserved. Except for brief quotations in critical articles or
reviews, no part of this book may be reproduced in any manner without
prior written permission from the publisher:

Black Lawrence Press
326 Bigham Street
Pittsburgh, PA 15211

Published 2013 by Black Lawrence Press, an imprint of Dzanc Books.
Printed in the United States

Acknowledgments

Poems in this work have originally appeared in *Bayou, Bellingham
Review, Crab Orchard Review, FIELD, The Florida Review, Memorious,
Ninth Letter, The Superstition Review,* and *Third Coast.*

For Ka

Contents

FOUR

Only what is human can truly be foreign.
The rest is mixed vegetation...
—Wislawa Szymborska

The one doubtful tree here
is the broom
—Robert Graves

Internal Organs of Murdered
Girl Received at University
—Headline, *The Urbana Daily Courier,*
Friday, April 28, 1922

The Cast

George Morrow:
Based on the first Dean of the College of Agriculture at the University of Illinois at Urbana-Champaign. In 1876, he established, with Professor of Agriculture Manley Miles, the Morrow Plots, a now-revered series of soil plots upon which agricultural experiments could be conducted. The Plots became a National Historic Landmark in May of 1968.

Manley Miles:
See: George Morrow

Sophia:
Greek Goddess of Wisdom

Chevreuil:
Early 19th-century French chemist said to have invented margarine.

Blackall:
Based on Clarence H. Blackall, the architect who, in the late 1800s, designed what was later to be dubbed Foellinger Auditorium, the intended nucleus of the University of Illinois.

Artie Clarke:
Based on Sir Arthur C. Clarke, author of 2001: A Space Odyssey.

Kepler:
Based on Johannes Kepler, a German astrologer, astronomer, and mathematician who, in the late 1500s–early 1600s, revised the previously-accepted laws of planetary motion.

Gert:

Based on Gertrude Hanna, a Central Illinois choirgirl who was murdered in 1922.

Alice:

A dual role: At times the name refers to an imagined version of a major donor to the University of Illinois's Alumni Association; at times the name refers to my sister.

Helene:

Based on Helene Foellinger, the daughter of an Indiana newspaperman. In 1932, she served as that paper's first female editor. In 1958, she began the Foellinger Foundation, which donated a large sum of money to the renovation of an auditorium on the University of Illinois campus that now bears her name.

ONE

The Morrow Plots

You sit on the roof
of the Biology Building, against

such a color green,
you don't know if it once

was copper, capable of boiling
or freezing

an egg. The book opening
to your knees

explodes with border scenes—
skeletal fish becoming women

with piñata faces.
When skin is cut

into strips like this, it can,
from a distance, be a beard,

a chapter about the half-life
of food. Below you,

one vegetable huddles
against another, evolving,

these incredible skins
unchewable, the worm

who finds its way in,
to fruit.

We must be peeled
to be eaten, under a roof

to find heat. And the jarred gods
of reptile and rock,

the way that, in the formaldehyde
suspension, we are all missing

links. That sound below you
is the corn talking,

to the cows, the agronomists,
the piñatas filled

with endless *huitlacoche*.
Up here, you can't tell

exactly who experiments and who
is experimented on.

When you wake on the roof
of a biology building, the stars

will be so affectionate
that you can't muster enough anxiety,

the temperature required
to boil water, to make more than

half of this life
astonishing.

Baphomet

Sophia escaped into corn today
to venerate wisdom

and the families who eat it
with holders.

She was chased by four college boys
who didn't dare jump

the fence, crack the code on the soles
of her feet. No time

for the emergency callbox,
the jangle of security.

In the rows, she could hear
the ocean,

imagine the scallops there, charred
on their flat tops and bottoms,

soft as wax in the middles. Under
her tongue, the sponge

of urchin, the orange brine
and sea vinegar,

the champagne that, by definition,
is heretical. On our lips,

still the flavors of an idol
and the human head,

wood gently smoking
our lives.

In wisdom is this code and worship,
the word that ends in *ss*. It is,

when spoken, the aperitif of escape,
the liver of God, the loved thing

that allows us our quickness and the right
to disappear

from drunk boys in open shirts,
every superhero

leaping for their lives from a torn breast
pocket. When we drop

our capes, we can't fly, differentiate
between what's salt

and what's pepper. Here, all voice
is not song,

the way the lip strains
to cover her teeth.

Someone will hear her comfort the stalks
and mistake it for a night wind

of specific hour, the flavors
of the Midwest making

boneyards of the sea. The soft give of all
red meat, the poaching

in fat, sweet cream and paprika.
We bite to hide

and taste to protect—our fingers
from burning at the tips,

the wisdom we lose
to eating.

Can you imagine being punched in the mouth?

Wildfire in Central Illinois

The blackened Morrow Plots,
experimental corn, never having
known shade. The Graduate Library

built underground so as not to cast
a shadow, this burial
of books, this shovel

of young minds looking
everything up—*ichthyology,
perspicacious, sex as social*

construct, the origin of the skirt.

Who, now, will boil us our dinner,
slather it with butter and salt?
Yesterday, a woman found

Chevreuil in the stacks, mistook him
for a pearl. As later reported, this
is a common thing with French chemists.

He was the first to boil water,
to write, *the first time you made love
to a woman named Margaret* ...

Yesterday, three boys took
off their clothes, ran through
the sacred fields, cutting themselves

on the silks. They thought, *in our blood
is a National Historic Landmark, a blow
to crop science.* Today, they are in jail,

a pair of red boxer shorts still tied
like a flag to the stalk. An oyster
to the Parisian . . .

The pirates are buried with the hooks
and books, their teeth having fallen
to corn. They blame the fire

on a six-year-old boy whose mother
insists it was an accident, his first time
playing with matches. She remembers

the day the Dewey Decimal System
died, her grandmother praying for corn
and a mortar, for a book

of matches to clutch her
in its skinny hand. This literary coffin:
she wonders if it can still

be eaten, studied. She prays for . . .

Winter is coming and things are burnt,
a polyp for the kernel,
a mouth for us all.

Chaff

for Alice

They ran and ran after me like smart
cows, knowing of the slaughter, hearing
the stories, I ran and ran from them

like a bullet they knew was retractable
into corn or
half of corn

it felt like a brass bed,
the one I had good dreams in
when I was nine, so much

more than the illusion
of a farm, covered in buildings,
classrooms, the small reek of a doll's

fake brown hair, silver crayon, lipstick
for girls,
time shot unoiled

from that sidewalk, the quad
barrel from Biology Building
to the corn

and when they finished, they had
their names written
in the newspapers from Savoy

to Chicago, but on different
pages, and I finally found the right
bar of soap and laughed and wept and

fell asleep
with striations on my hands
among the empty cobs.

Parlor-cum-Pasture

Scatter of cows—batteries of imprecise
calves, planted near the clothesline.

Impressed
and surgical. Healthy cows

butterfly stroke home
from Wichita, but they're acting.
They're always successful.

They embrace, these calves,
their killers. Publish
calf secrets—

everything in their hide
concealing the impala

genetics, the antelope
will comfort them.

The cows are clean with beginning.
Bulls goose-step
with other bulls

selecting which for meat,
which for milk.
The saddest cows

look for the lost saddle. Leave everyone alone.
If anyone brings their crop to the creek,

they will know the cows
can not be baited.

Instead, they eat a red turtleneck,
figuratively, the turtle,
because the meaters know

that contrast can be bloody.
Then, the milkers will dream
of a plow that tills

the stuff inside them.

"Suggestive to the Practical Farmer"

—George E. Morrow

An ear, mismanaged, bends
at the end, a broken finger,
a meal ungranted. Before this land,

the shovel's breaking into sepia
soil and well-dressed ditch-diggers
who ignore the camera,

we would only produce
30 bushels an acre, not enough
to keep the red knuckles

from our doors, a juggling
of plains and bells.
The wife of Manley Miles

held his kisses beneath dirt,
a nightstand drawer growing
encyclopedias in deep, black prairie . . .

The same field couldn't
possibly keep up, this hateful
corn swims in kerosene.

We have to read by another light,
dig by fog and by morning. Severe
rotational starving...

Our hands once filled
with the filth that would feed us.
How could they know

that Plots One and Two
would be replaced by an Observatory—
that Mars could become

more important than eating?
A volcano and six years of alternates:
corn-corn-oats-meadow-meadow-

meadow. This is how we survive:
in nightgowns and clover,
alfalfa burning the 1800s

and the sadness of the soybean.
My father made his living
from the stars, the lime reserved

for Cygnus, and the lens through which
corn becomes sanctuary
to the thief. In this nutrition

is a new way to read at night,
a way to feel alive in our chests.
Sometimes, this involves reading

about lambs on the roof of a school,
building a planet from the sound
of a lightswitch. Sometimes,

this involves phosphorus
and the calf of a girl
who will never be their wives.

There is nothing about the comet
that is suggestive to the practical farmer
and a new generation of students

who feed on Illinois. What would George
say to Manley Miles?
That the Book of the Dead

is written on boiling water?
That our tomes must shrivel
like snails to salt?

What can we do
but eat them? Imagine them yellow,
imagine the farmer chained to his star

studying us
pull dream from the lamp,
heart by the fistful.

The Transfiguration of the Aardvark

Arguably, the aardvark
rests beneath the soil
studying astronomy

and agriculture.

It plants itself out
of prehistory into
this field, where

boys and girls listen

to a lecture about
phosphorus, its green
powder form, its place

in America's salt shaker.

We must use anything
we can get our hands on
to flavor our food, bloating

from kernel to whale,

this water runs
so elegantly
from an exoskeleton,

hard-plating an earth

in dwarfdom. The animal
log-rolls in its sleep
and one corn stalk

leans against another.

One girl will think
of lovers on a beach
on an island that begins

with the letter P,

of slackening foreheads,
as the professor unbuttons
the soil with a thumbtip,

reduces a meal to its seed.

The boy next to her
will drop his red notebook,
that night drink too much whiskey

and watch the stars die.

A page with
an early airplane
whips in the wind.

Only in an experimental cornfield

can we get away
with such romanticism,
can the aardvark

cloak itself in silk,

hold its breath for this long.
In evolution is long
long hair. This,

like the dirt

burning at the mantle,
is inarguable.

On Seeing a U.F.O. Land in the Cornfield

1.

Twenty-two in Merry Ann's Diner tonight,
the coffee there to keep us

warm and awake. We saw this thing happen
in the Plots, something to do with the last

crumb of dream, its spice, white pepper folded
into cream. We saw shirts whip like sails,

buttons scream open, this alien protecting
its nipples with some kind of hand. We were

a collection of hands clasped together
flattening God between our palms.

This whole thing so decidedly unidentified,
the whimpers and rustle, the threshing

going on down in the dirt. We were none
so tall to see over the corn

to the husks made separate, to the fodder,
the membrane, the strange clothes ripping, the brittle bracts...

We did nothing. Not even for the sake
of an inflorescence. Three or four

of them. They looked
to be made of dogwood.

Now, it will take a train
trailing scarves of wind to hold us

together, the needle and the thread,
sewing this myth into corn, a slack

open-legged acceptance into an article—
the police blotter and the second page.

In the stars we saw jealousy,
saw the collar high on the butterfly.

We write our declaration on its wings
and anything else we suspect

will fly away.

2.

This has nothing to do with the arrangement
of stars, how one shot

like a slow bullet, our alarm clocks
going off at once, the bluegrass station

struggling to rename our bedrooms
Lily. She was hurt,

though she didn't seem it.
She was the first to report it

to the papers, the first to be
laughed off. The corn is there only

for thesis statements, topic sentences.
Afterward, we heard that the grounds crew

sprayed the vegetables, a decontaminant
as thin as a sheet—pink on a brass bed,

a little blood in the dirt—they spray
to stuff the noses of the moths,

this chemical scarecrow, through
the funnel of night, its hair,

its hair through the funnel.

3.

You think this means that evolution
is over, that all vapor will regress

to its original sea. You say, *those fucking
college boys ruined us. That*

fucking girl... But we saw
what we saw.

You said, pointing to the roof
of the auditorium as it fell, *This cloud*

has flippers. Later, we opened our
textbooks, found the diner, renamed

ourselves Jason, that argonautical
son of a bitch, choking on centuries

of fleece.

4.

We dream of Colchis and of California,
of 1849 and the comforts

of a gold-flecked counter, a diner
waffle and diner ice cream. We repeat:

it was a U.F.O. It dropped like a penny,
picked itself up. There was nothing impressive

about its breath. Inside the corn,
we heard the scrambling of horses'

hearts beating too fast, a groan.
Then, the tracks behind the diner,

the spoons singing, suddenly
locomotive, and we saw lights

bright as water on whale skin.
This is the shape of the ship, the algebra

of hope. In the words *prepare, prepare…*
We wonder what their names are,

if they know the corn is alive, that ears
are an old joke.

On the interstate, not a single truck
overturns, the oils and grains

shifting. In the sound of air-brakes,
we draw our conclusions

that a winter is coming, that this story
ends on ice. We realize how all engines

are alien.

5.

They don't want to die on this planet,
are afraid of our water and fire,

this flying saucer, collecting
the spills, the warrior missing

his wife, and the two dogs who forgot
their leashes, peeling their lips

like oranges, the color of dirty sheets,
of split olives, they spit their socks

and wet, plush rabbits, pace mad
wishing that instead of labs,

these buildings had living rooms, rugs
to lie on, fireplaces, that this scaffolding

indicated not wreckage, but a dreamhouse
uplifted from the freezing puddles

that kill the corn, these octopus hallways,
the deliberate shadow arms of the cat,

her fight stopping.

6.

One door after another opens.
No one said, "Take me."

TWO

Life Sciences

When the corn is painted with the most
exotic thing we can imagine—
a goat, perhaps, or
the blood of the goat—clench your fists
to your chest, mimic
the chambers of the heart.
In this, you show your fear
at being the object of another's
initiation into the patch-worthy,
a symbol to carry us
from these copper roofs going green,
all the first edition textbooks stinking
like steampipes.

Your knees, of course, will pull
to your chest—brain, this time.
Anything with a lobe.
Between them, you see all the other girls,
their skinny ribs draped
as if in documentary, all those things
behind glass in Life Sciences
and you realize something about protection,
that you don't have to be an embryo
to be amphibious, to be young
and crumpled by the side of the train tracks
with the rest of them, found
out past the diner, their bodies covered
in fine moss.

Shame on this earth for being fertile
for giving us food that never rejects
the sun. The pack animals here
run on diesel, and bring the air
down to our level, where we can breathe it.

If I wasn't so far away, I would
offer you my hand, call us
what we are:
a species that finds
even our own blood
revolting.

Manley's Fever Lament

I'm upset with George
but more concerned with Alice
who assured us last night
she was fleeing the state.
I don't care if my name
dies without illuminant

if, before leaving, she picks all
the dandelions from the lawn.
Her dress is so quiet
just as dumb as the experiment
I dreamt last night and then thought
was ingenious—

repeating corn
without clover,
shucking themselves incessantly
and spitting milk at their shadows,
this madman corn going cross-eyed
in the dark windows

of the corpse-green auditorium.
It seems that a few students
are coming to ask questions . . .
and dumb, dumb, because the heart
is just another fist
Alice is shocked is still beating

she'll crumple her dress
onto the floor and kick it
until they see Quincy and Monticello,
our Dobermans with dissolving hips
swallowing someone's liver
wrapped in a paper bag on the road shoulder.

It's not their fault. We never
meant it to be this way.
For 1922 to be so depressing.
The paper sacks were supposed
to protect the corn from squirrels
and birds, keep the kernels
from seeing—every
ripening thing deserves
protection—not to conceal

a murder. God, Alice,
can't you wait to leave?
Think of that poor choirgirl
from Hoopeston, how the newspaper said
she *met her death*
while her betrayer attempted

to force her to undergo
an illegal operation. Words
like *marriage* and *lover*
followed by *overdose*
of chloroform. Her body hidden
on a shelf in the parsonage cellar

of the Presbyterian Church,
the morning shift carpenters
finding her, their hands holding
like mosquitoes above
a pond of hammers. If we pick
the right chemical, no one

gets malaria. Not today.
They think, Alice, it was a widower.
A retired farmer. The Plots,
that night, could not
provide her solace. I should tell this
to George.

And a farmer like that,
a man who once was married,
treating the body like testimony . . .
Who cares if my wife
wears silk to bed, keeps an almanac
in the nightstand drawer?

In the fields, there's only
other love, and the birds
make corpses of the cobs.
So many dead things, so soon
after having been born. Who cares
if the clover is wilting,

or that my wife plays both sides
of the chessboard in her nightgown

while I'm fast asleep, making up
songs about a woman
named Alice? Alice
is losing her mind anyway,

and her thin coat-hanger
bones reinforce my right to dream—
in it, now, our house
is on top of the soil,
the living room sprouting
thirteen millers who spew

the prettiest lavender
invective, but I'm innocent,
as I always am, planting only
edibles into a cattailed bog—where once
a small girl turned all
her goldfish loose...

Her dog was old and toothless,
some of the goldfish were blind.

Types of Symphony

When the sun rises behind the black

                                    cow, everything

around the cow brightens. This

is the rule. The milk pails

upturned by the night,
the river, the landowner in bed

                              biting his lip. No one is exempt. The wife

who has pulled their daughter awake
by her hair. In her scalp, needlemarks

                                    of blood struggle

against her skin, nothing
                      a hairbrush can fix,
nothing to undo the knot.
I don't know what to make of this

                             as I wake next to you,

your neck steeped in days-old panache,
the kind of perfume a shower

does nothing to wash away. I can't tell
if the cow is a sign of doom

                    or hope,

if the landowner's teeth
are too weak to break the skin.

                                        Your answer isn't
an answer at all, but more
of an aubade, your fingers, in sleep, reaching
                                                for the piano

in the blankets,

your voice like the cow's to the world
                                        to every hairbrush
not picked up, to the boy who,

in the back of a barn,

handles his first gun. Sleep,
like some rough draft of God
                                still engaged in the nonviolent

act of dove-making.

Ave

The first pictures of you
in a pumpkin patch
and with sunglasses
the first time

you stain your thumbnail
with black ink, discover
that some things don't
come out for days, even

if you cry. I wish you saw
your grandmother slipping
chervil into your formula—
her car totaled in the Navy Yard,

barely Chicago, her second
husband arrested behind
barbed wire and a Ferris wheel,
forgiven over . . .

We are always trying to prove
we're not Midwestern,
but the peanut shells on the soles
of our shoes give us away.

My sister has just eaten
the best meal of her life.

I can't believe it includes
habañero pepper. You should

know this: even the dogs
love you, and forgive
your age, that the heart
can not grow a moustache

or anything close
to fatherly. That you are safe
only when glossy, a music box
of 19th century spoons

allowing you sleep and cereal,
something orange and sweet.
Here, tarnish is copper
and therefore, valuable.

In your hands, not a single
quiet stain, your room,
a breaking microphone.
Here, the baby toys of the world

slit their throats, silent,
not dangerous, and all too glass.
They, and we, want to be
so animate when grown up,

lit from the inside, and carved
into. A hole for the candle,
a slate for a face.

Breadbasket

I have not eaten for days.
It is common—this notion of what happens
under each tooth.
A coven of molecules burning
with the wet hay of the harvest.
As I chew on the air, I feel, under my
shirt, the metal cold
of a dying girl's hands.

When the diner reopens, I will eat,
visit my friends in the hospital,
a sick doctor losing himself
in the fluorescent light
while shaving the chest
of a broken farmer.

On an empty stomach,
there is a fullness to sitting on the roof
of a building dedicated to the study of life,
the wet-eyed edges of things
that could be the falling of a student chorus,
could be the corn
gently blown, the statue
of a Huguenot lost in Illinois.
Up here, strangely un-hungry,
height and food have fused. My body,
this thick bag for transience.

Into Snow

In this, these taillights, the most
red emanation of God, or an apple—

something with a substantial
core—we follow a funeral procession,

the hearse putting into our mouths
the word we gum, but don't speak.

Death, again. We can't believe it
and, in not believing, the ghost

keeps obviously warm.
At the edge of the interstate,

crows subvert the corn, revise
the stomachs of the entire Midwest

with very little flapping,
these black bobbins swish final

and low, making puppets
of the stalks. You are the one

to turn the radio off, a former
gangster from Kankakee talking

about how poetry saved his life.
Strange how, in the middle

of the farms, the convenience stores
still hide behind bulletproof glass.

You are the one who read
the article about all the victims here

and their running, their opulent
donations to the university,

about how, one day, it's Fall,
the next, Winter. When the hearse

brakes before us, we imagine
we can hear the corpse

shifting, that the shredded
truck tires on the shoulder

are two Dobermans baring
their teeth. Something is angry

at us for being here. A heart,
perhaps, missing

the soft bed of its chest.
We get the feeling that this

is a place where so many people
misplaced the orthodoxy of love,

left alone in the inside pocket
of last year's goosedown coat.

The crumpled mittens
still wet at the wrists.

The braking is always sudden.
I would have reached

for your hand. A crow drops dead
bounces from the roof

of the hearse. The smallest
crash. Forgive me

for veering off the road
into snow. I was only trying

to look at the cows.

THREE

Des Plaines

We ford the river with red construction paper.

Here, dalliance

is a virtue: a little glue,

a little glitter . . .

We can make adulthood an octopus,
put it in the mouth

of a seven-story gargoyle.

Like I told you, you should
see this: the wastebasket

filled with medication samples, the last inch

of your first joint, hair

and the yearbook page with
your old boyfriend's message: something
about a Michael,

something about a braid.

When radiated, the milkweed tires, tries,
can't produce for even the skinniest

of nieces. The new one.
Let's cut her a leopard-skin cape

and pink hood from this catalog.

Let's cut her matching mittens. Make her
a collage that can heal.

                              I don't mind when
you vomit into the water.
On the outer bank, a redbird
                              on an electrical box

pecking at the padlock.

I don't mind. The instructions are inside.

International Symbol of Welcome

Broken in 1877, Blackall
called the witches to meet

beneath the oculus, already
glass and vestibular. They said

he even had the heart
of an architect, maintained

by scaffolding, rib, and the pulse
of two-thousand plus signs.

A year earlier, he fell off
the roof of the tool shed,

what was later to become
Lincoln Hall, its lectures

on mythology, cardboard
lightning, and the women

gathered to him all forcemeat
and gray braids. They healed

his compound fractures, shuffled
bone as if cards, jacks torn

at their corners, demanded
in return, that the roof bear

a copper pineapple—the broomstick
version of open arms. On the lawn,

they collected in petition
their favorite pictures

from empty vases, the proverbial
naked man who receives

from four shrouded women
his eyes and teeth and something

that looks like a pie. Behind
this image, the sky smoked,

alder and burning vegetable,
a ribbon cutting . . .

When the building went up
and cast such a voluptuous

shade, George Morrow fell
to his knees and offered the last

untouched ear, raw as a pencil
and sugar. On his mother's birthday,

he banished all women
and physicists from the Plots,

each punished for using
infant subjects to study

the acoustics of the auditorium.
Here, the tallest, most central

figure always makes the largest
donation. She takes off her cloak,

insists that Babel is buried
somewhere in Central Illinois,

that its Muse is built from the salts
of the unborn, stuffed into cornhusks

and sewn with Archaea, every
ingredient found in the refrigerators

of the Biology Building, behind
the blackbirds. Helene

gifted their bodies back
to the school, and removed

the extra skylight. Now,
the pineapple calls to the stars

a welcome more interstellar
than international, no matter

how rotten or barbarous. The field
that serves as its gateway

is the fire-pit to Blackall's
blueprints, all design falling

into the lap of one young student,
sacrificed to fruit, the healthy prostates

of those boys who refuse
to design. What can we do

but disguise ourselves as beasts—
the hare in red leaves, the fish

in the ice storm, bird when the flies
find the crop, and corn come summer

when their eggs hatch?
We give ourselves to the mouths

of greyhounds, the bitch-otter,
the falcon, the solar black

of the hen. Somewhere,
behind skirts and feathers,

all tested infants shed
their combs, weep so we can hear

the architecture of our bodies
collapsing under this dolmen earth.

Vesper

Biology is in the organs,
she says, a bargained

huddle into one corner.
We were born here

in a circling of the body's
wagons. Dying is different, muddy,

its thin film colder, a sheet
of butter over too much bread—in shivering feet

is all this time to think
about the vegetation in the sink

that betrays you, feeds you
then eats you

alive. It allows so many boys
to unbutton their shirts, the joy

of cloth swinging open has its own
ballad, like a glass cabinet, the mown

topography of such fertile soil.
Together, we bring to a boil

the descending melodic contour.
Lipstick, in such cases, is a bore,

she says, poorly applied,
such a red mess, messed wide,

describing the heart that once held such
responsibility inside her, the touch

her mother called *gold.*
But ascension, she stresses, is cold

and harp-less, only a shattered wind
forced through the holes pinned

in our lids. This is supposed to be
mercy, she clarifies, but the car key

to the spirit can't have too much fun
in a mason jar, eating into one

green leaf. At least
they went to jail, I say, but she

only whistles—I can't tell
if its her breath or the smell

of the weather, winter
coming, the banter

of snow tinkling like a xylophone
struck with butter knives, a drone-

song that can't slow itself down
or go quiet, a sound

that keeps, like a cure, playing.

Woodwind

This wind makes a saxophone
of the chimney

and you sit against it
on a copper roof

under which boys and girls
keep warm with smocks,

protect their eyes
with plastic goggles.

You found out early:
it's not so easy to dissolve

powder into liquid.
The pages of so many books

reassert themselves, the words
meaningful even when wet.

One told the story of the farmer
who beat his pigs

with cornstalks, the ones who
couldn't bear food,

the sows roaring, their ears
confused. You remember this

as you open the red envelope,
here, above the farms, brick

and pipes the only topography,
read the expensive card

your mother sent you
about complications

with your sister's pregnancy.
The one nurse who kissed

her eyes. The snapping down
of her legs and practiced dialogue,

forgotten lines, scraps of her
collected with cotton, lab slips

and paper bills, a revision
of root (*that's ok, that's ok*)

and mirrors, the body
as conquered husk,

something for bad dreams
to summit, and a heavy

green sweater . . .
All important things

no bigger than a thumbnail,
the breaking of a cordial glass

onto a kitchen floor
covered with wings.

There is nothing
these pigeons can do

except roost against the chimney
and act warm.

The Doges of Urbana

The pigeons fly in untied patterns
over the auditorium's rooftop pineapple—
a sailboat swaddled in a briar patch . . .
They come together, targeting
the gray sky, dropping curtains of wind

over the church wheelbarrow on which
the maimed choirgirl, just last night,
dreamt of roses.

We can blame these pigeons,
arrowing this unshaded corn,
for lending life to the screamless
stretcher. We can blame
the importance of food and books—libraries
plowed to make fields, fields burned
to make laboratories—for these boys
who experiment with soil, find themselves
naked in front of mirrors, hurt their thumbs
while cutting others, for doctors
who, coming across acres
of perfect dirt, can only
pronounce:

the names of the farmers who use
tractors as warships, scissors in place
of surgeons with smooth hair,

dismounting to poke holes
in the flagship girls, calling them names
and setting them to burn, while Morrow
and Miles slice deep into beefsteak tomatoes . . .

Within a shed that has never seen
so much manure, the erection
of meal to plate.
In their honor, one farmer
will feel the urge to amputate
with a sponge and needle, things
not sharp enough to sow.
He will gather planets of thread
and a saucer of heated paraffin.
He will stitch with an old
silk stocking.

In following years, many boys
and girls will be dead, and this girl
is scarcely alive, the young farmer's face
orange like a night tornado,
collecting its power from the few
hissing streetlamps—this sodium dustbowl,
the earth lit with beating coals.

The handsaw doesn't work
as well as he hoped, his hands now
the color of fresh brick,
an old photograph of the carriage
upon which his grandfather stored

his guns and cowhide. His hands
begin to hurt, the incision
hidden in the shadows—a sweet
granted darkness, the thing
Morrow and Miles stripped from the earth
in the name of production.
So we can eat what the farmer can't,
but only underground
can we read.

This one: his thumbnail falls
into the friction of the cutting
where the whole body
is arterial. Above him, the pigeons
draw their dark wings over their breasts
in ridicule, and a wind carries them
further into the sky.

The dying girl is from Kankakee.
What she had to endure! Morrow
once told Miles that a winter tornado
was good for the corn, the snow,
in effect, was the tiller. Her sister
worked for Urbana Industrial Paper
Manufacture and Letterpress Printing,
a girl with tiny fingers
leaning with her shoulders
into levers made of lead,
the falling icon
of an interminable bouquet—ferns

and baby's breath—inked
onto still-wet paper, its pulp
like sour mash, the Prohibition
pipeline run from Hoopeston
to Chicago.

Her sister, a woman of hinges,
crushed first by the levers,
could only find sleep
in intoxicants. The pipeline
that ran alcohol under the Mississippi
held her body in tight secret
for fifty-seven years.
Illinois named
a mile of interstate
after her.

Their nephew, Artie Clarke,
found their lives
in newspaper archives,
dreamt of their delicate machinery
as supercomputers in the corn.

He will tell his grandmother, *Ma,*
she was no innocent.
She was an inmate
at the Kankakee Hospital
for the Insane. If she hadn't
been killed, she would have
killed herself. Remember:

we have no sea here—
we have to build it from keys
and a screen, lend intelligence
to salt, an ocean that knows
how to survive in the soil, to wait
like a window, for summer
or the heat of the wood stove
to fool the seasons, my glasses opaque
with soot. I can see the girls
bound at the ankles every time
I put them on . . .

Pulling from his grandmother's
heavy arms, Clarke studies
the acoustics of the train tracks
and the cars
from the roof of Topper's Pizza, smells
undercooked dough and the meadow
that comes with it. What miracles!

This is the first time he's seen
annuals flowering from the street curbs
in winter, the people gathering in disbelief
look to him, white as teeth,
cut as the harvest. He wonders why
piles of burning cobs don't fill
with air like the accordion, why they
keep their music
to themselves.

He wants reason, wants to see
ants in the snow lighting tiny fires,
their bodies, bellows. Jars of black whiskey
made from the husks, leaking
like gasoline from their lids.
Everything milled treated with lime!

A biology student will follow him
home, that night, in her diary,
write of his genius and the breadth
of his chest, the things named HAL
that must live there. In the morning,
a birthing cow will step on her thigh,
the wound hidden in the shadow
of her blue stocking. The horseflies
that find her, will be so young.

She knows: there are meetings in the fields,
women bare to the knees
in the snow, massaging an ecstatic wind
with twigs and frozen leaves.

They cut their hair
with stolen pencil sharpeners, offer it—brown,
yellow, red—to the pigeons, their bodies
so white, this earthbound constellation
shooting and shooting.

Halos of breath become
tornadoes, the struggle of a handsaw

blowing away, open shirts blowing
closed, the pants of angry boys
refastening, their eyes swollen shut
to blacklights, their purple hands
open, frosted and accepting. Clarke,

out of state now, spits pipe tobacco
into a rain puddle, and names
a computer after its sound.
He trembles at the ripped reflection
of crackable headstones. The sound

is the sound of the fields,
the bald women who have warmed
the birds, the corn in watercolor
that can not grow,
but will always be abundant.
Like the rose in a dead girl's dream,
dropping its petals into the obese lungs
of the printing press,

our lesson is learned
from weather and George Morrow,
his tenacity, the honoring
of the smallest things,
food
and wedding rings.
There are mice
threading the pages of their almanacs,
cuttings everywhere

and thick blankets shrouding
the kitchen tables.

It was the liver
out-beating the heart. Gert, it was
the newspaperman calling your clothes
disarranged, your wounds, *marks*.

It was losing your legs
to an ill-equipped farmer
who had no business
with anesthetics,
your daughter's flat mouth
piping your milk to the sky,
the stars' white lanterns, the infant
like a sail, buried in the sharpest part
of the central garden.

All we know
is that everyone lived for a few more years.

Autoerotic Asphyxiation

The world goes pink with buffoonery,
billions of squirrels

running away. In their cheeks
acorns arrange themselves

like dog stars, wait
for the constellation

that looks like a camel.
A mesquite jealousy

in humplessness, the stockings
we save for just such an occasion.

We haven't spent
this much time here

since we were seventeen,
when mortality was a barking sky,

an animal a continent away,
this documentary

about Morocco. Like the squirrels
we move without headlights.

You speak equations
into my ear that would take

the stocking to solve.
Canicula. Ligature. In the next

room, we hear my father's
one sharp cough, wonder

if we're not breathing
enough.

Row, Row

In the park, the child falls
                          from her rhinoceros.
A Russian nanny lifts her from the woodchips

by a cotton hood.

We watch this through two red telescopes,
the rowboat gentling
                          the river.

Even from this distance, you say,
you can distinguish cotton
                          from other cloth,

a gnat from a star. We talk
                          about your family, my family,
strokes and sore throats.
A miscarriage
                    pulled by horses, a sister riding

behind. The stream, evaporating, becomes
the chamomile tea she needs at night.

Above us, life is
but the osprey fighting off the Canada goose.
                                    In the nests,

a pulled sound, babyish
horrible, the goat not yet dead

                              stretched into a drum,
the tea steam wishing itself
a geyser. Or a dream—
                    of a rhinoceros

detached from its spring, its horns
finding our mothers' arms

exotically jungled, where the medicine
goes in, merrily.
                    (The things that push us down

are big enough to house us).
                              The little girl knows
(we imagine we watch

her knowing) those things in the trees

could be tap shoes or bloodbats.
That thing the goose trips over

                              is the island.

FOUR

Kepler's Last Law

The gargoyles with their frosted hair
guard the entrance to the library.

They are brother and sister, coffee-
stained, their muscular necks, things

under which teenagers still kiss
reaching up with flapping fingers

to write their names. From below,
my sister tells me, a fang is only

a small circle, a picture of the sun
in the central color pages

of a children's book about astronomy—
the one my mother bought me,

my seventh birthday, hoping
I would go into the sciences,

unearth the skull of some Midwestern
dinosaur, polish it like a pearl.

Tell her that, in every cornfield,
is an ellipse that cries when it moos.

This is, after all, a law
of conservation, the orbit of her hand

as she bakes mandelbrot with chocolate chips
for the holidays, the finished scones

cooling on a sheet pan subject
to the hard gravitation

of room temperature. Their smoke
loses itself in the space of a yellow

chandelier, the small extinction
of heat. My sister,

angry after I dropped her
dollhouse family down the bathroom sink,

burned my book in the snow,
the chapter on Mars having outlasted

the fattest of the Jovians, the unspeakable
cold of the milk. I knew even then

that she changed my life,
that my heart was not a good one—

a silk handkerchief, a bony
hand—an argument with genetics

I could not win, my body
stubbornly Aristotelian, still believing that it,

like the Earth used to be, was a fulcrum.
(Kepler knows: here, an eraser is hard

to come by).
This pressure on my throat,

tightening now as I turn my back
on food, pass into pages, must be

my daughter, unborn, writing her name
on my breath.

Somewhere, in warm, warm kitchens . . .

The hardest thing the Earth asks of us,
with its smells of white flour, requires

not the tractor, but remembering.

Offering

Because the floorboards
are mopped with chill

and the arms of the orange chairs
lay open with offering,

gold or Florida can exist
only in thick wool,

Illinois asserting itself
with dead vegetables,

the green thumbs cut off
with hedge-trimmers

and piled into garages with the seed.
We fertilize ourselves

with experiment, tomatoes
the size of our heads,

everything about last summer's
murder used to kindle the fire.

No one told us the girl's name
or the jacket sizes

of the boys who almost
got away with it. They wanted

to be scientists, each one,
the permanent red ink

of discovery on their fingertips.
No one told us

that raw newsprint smells
like our sweat,

all of our water held back now,
dammed into skin. You say

it depends on the nature
of the article . . .

But even you know
the students are on vacation,

the field stripped of importance
and fast heartbeat. Just a dry

broom, swept into wind.
This morning, over coffee,

what you say, you could say
about the entire state. *This is*

a cold house.

For Weather

The diner is closed today
for weather, a paper sign

on the door, the parking lot
unplowed, the trains

derailed at Mason City
because of the ice. That noise

could have been deer
folding into the fields

while the Monticello
Boys Choir sang

in the auditorium
about messenger angels. But what

is ceremony without coffee,
pancakes wet with butter,

frozen blueberries, spatulas
greased with this morning's

eggs, while someone crouches
outside in corn, hiding prayer

beneath her blue sweatshirt,
the whispers of farm

against farm, conspiring
to unzip Illinois?

The same man who
discovered margarine

named his daughter
after a white flower.

In the south garden,
bearing his name, the cows

lose their legs in deep snow,
eating down to the exhausted grass

and the frozen lowing things
that uphold it. In this,

we find our can openers
and turn the heat so high,

the air filling with such expectation
it could be the new year.

No Bells in Tuscola

In the middle of December,
something rings

in the corn, the bull's eye
of campus, in a blue light

that is three-quarters
at best,

tracks me like a sister
into a world of developing

bells. Husks
pull closed over dying meat.

A dusky tongue gongs
the lips of liberty

and Andromeda is pushed
to the sky's orange rim.

The barntops hide
from the roofs of libraries

and labs, inhabit this season
with humble angles

acute against the night
and the things that sleep

in it. In St. Joseph,
a television is turned off,

a bed goes dark.
In Mahomet, a woman checks

to see if a window is closed
because how can this house

be so drafty? Her feet drag
slowly across the carpet

gathering enough electricity
to fill a glass with warm water

from the tap, the faucet
closing like a curtain

in a hospital where
so many babies, just today

were born. Somewhere—
Tuscola, maybe—we all

reach an age when we stop
crying over trivial things

and words, where blessings
fall to asphalt and melt.

Under the cornfield,
the Boneyard Creek

hatches its fish in secret,
waiting for the philanthropist

moon to lift
its water up.

Illinois Witches

Broom of hackberry,
dormancy on the lawn.

We don't yet realize
we can eat the mildew,

test the buds
for their sugar.

Where the corn is now, sixteen women
were slaughtered with a scythe in 1806,
the symptoms of sweetness and a burlap rope.
They used farming as an excuse . . .

We all die forward,
the multiplex in Savoy

lighting our bloods
in pink. Up close,

we look like the short-twigs
of some secondary plant.

The men who laid this field
lit their oil and read how, throughout the Midwest,
the softest of the mites tie themselves
in the shoots, lay their eggs in May.

They read and rename
auditoriums after the breasts

of their founders' wives.
We have since been looking

for a broom-free species.
The reports call us, *aesthetically unpleasant.*

Until they sprayed us with sulfur,
we had food on our plates, barrettes
in our hair. We saw the star in the oak wilt.
Imagined the tunnel that, one day, boys

must walk through
after their classes,

ignoring the plots,
all the way to the Locust

Street tracks. We give them
peanut shells on the bottoms

of their shoes, beetles in their hands.
We give them their long walk,
a fucking sunset before them, trains
on either side.

Antebellum

The tornado inside Andromeda laid seeds
of clover in the sky. We took the stubble
and dissolved it in red wine, went into
the basement of the Genomic Biology Building
for asylum.

Helene had gone to a funeral that Sunday—
the body of her first lover covered
in tobacco. She said
that in burial
the screws of the corpse meet a pressure
of any blood not cleaned out,
they shoot into dirt like seeds. The arms
quickly flare like a chicken's,
and in the downdraft of soil
the teeth clench as if to keep
the earth out. He was finally rhetorical, she said.

Ernie spat on the floor, unwrapped the stolen corn
from the napkin, saying, "You saw
no such thing, Helene." When I was small,
Helene said, I stood with my father
at Mount Hope Cemetery. He was fresh
with mint and antebellum. The crops
were rotting because of the windy season,
we pricked our fingers and let them drip
onto newspaper. Alice, in a complicated

white dress, with the tornado dropping,
feigned a seizure and wiped
her cheek through the blood.
The rows of clay idols watched

and started to tip in the wind. Over us,
these shuddering memorials:
A rooster smothering a swallow
and behind us, two dogs

tugging-of-war with a chrysalis,
and an angel cradling a squirrel
between her breasts. She watched
the rooster tie the swallow in a knot
and in the quake, began
to step over the wind like a plot.

Photo by Nathan Putens

Matthew Gavin Frank is the author of *Preparing the Ghost: An Essay Concerning the Giant Squid and the Man Who First Photographed It* (forthcoming from Sarabande Books), *Pot Farm* (The University of Nebraska Press/Bison Books), *Barolo* (The University of Nebraska Press), *Warranty in Zulu* (Barrow Street Press), *Sagittarius Agitprop* (Black Lawrence Press), and the chapbooks *Four Hours to Mpumalanga* (Pudding House Publications), and Aardvark (West Town Press). Recent work appears in *The New Republic, The Huffington Post, Field, Epoch, AGNI, The Iowa Review, Seneca Review, DIAGRAM, Black Warrior Review, The Normal School, Crazyhorse, Indiana Review, North American Review, Pleiades, Crab Orchard Review, The Best Food Writing, The Best Travel Writing, Creative Nonfiction, Prairie Schooner, Hotel Amerika, Gastronomica*, and others. He was born and raised in Illinois, and currently teaches Creative Writing in the MFA Program at Northern Michigan University, where he is the Nonfiction Editor of *Passages North*. This winter, he prepared his first batch of whitefish-thimbleberry ice cream.